INSTANT JAPANESE

Completely
Phoneticized
For Instant Use!

Other Books by Boye Lafayette De Mente

INSTANT
JAPANESE

Everything You Need
in 100 Key Words

Boye Lafayette De Mente

YENBOOKS

YENBOOKS are published
by Tuttle Publishing, Japan

LCC Card No. 93-60054
ISBN 4-900737-07-0

First edition, 1993
Eighth printing, 2000

Printed in Singapore

Contents

Preface

A little language goes a long way!
It is a well-established fact that most people of average intelligence and education use a vocabulary of only five or six hundred words in going about their daily affairs. The reason for this, of course, is that it is possible to express a variety of thoughts by using various forms of a single word. Each additional word exponentially increases the number of thoughts one can express. Another obvious reason why a limited vocabulary is enough to get most people through a day is because they are primarily involved in basic situations that are repeated day after day.

The Japanese language is especially flexible because there are so many "set" expressions found in common, everyday situations. One can, for example, express over ten complete thoughts by using the different forms of a single Japanese verb. Mastering just ten verbs and their forms therefore makes it possible to say over one hundred things.

This handy guide is designed to show how a very small vocabulary is enough to quickly and fluently communicate over 1,000 ideas in Japanese. And because Japanese can be easily rendered into English phonetics, virtually all problems with pronunciation can be eliminated.

Instant Japanese contains a phoneticized pronunciation guide and all the key words and expressions you need to cover most of the personal situations you are likely to encounter during a brief visit to Japan.

How to
Pronounce Japanese

The Japanese language is very easy to pronounce. It is made up of precise syllables that are based on just five vowel sounds: *a* (ah as in hah), *i* (ee as in free), *u* (oo as in boo), *e* (eh as in met), and *o* (oh as in so). When consonant sounds are added to these vowel sounds, syllables are created which follow the same sound pattern: *ka* (kah), *ki* (kee), *ku* (koo), *ke* (kay), *ko* (koe), and *sa* (sah), *shi* (she), *su* (sue), *se* (say), *so* (soe), and so forth.

All you have to do to pronounce these syllables (and the words they make up) correctly, is to voice them according to the phonetics taught in this book. When you pronounce the Japanese words and phrases phonetically, the sounds come out "in Japanese."

Here are all of the syllables that make up the sounds in the Japanese language, along with their approximate phonetic equivalents.

A	I	U	E	O
ah	ee	oo	eh	oh
KA	**KI**	**KU**	**KE**	**KO**
kah	kee	koo	kay	koe
SA	**SHI**	**SU**	**SE**	**SO**
sah	she	sue	say	so
TA	**CHI**	**TSU**	**TE**	**TO**
tah	chee	t'sue	tay	toe
NA	**NI**	**NU**	**NE**	**NO**
nah	nee	noo	nay	no
HA	**HI**	**FU**	**HE**	**HO**
hah	he	who	hay	hoe
MA	**MI**	**MU**	**ME**	**MO**
mah	me	moo	may	moe
YA		**YU**		**YO**
yah		yoo		yoe
RA	**RI**	**RU**	**RE**	**RO**
rah	ree	rue	ray	roe
GA	**GI**	**GU**	**GE**	**GO**
gah	ghee	goo	gay	go
ZA	**ZI**	**ZU**	**ZE**	**ZO**
zah	jee	zoo	zay	zoe
DA	**JI**	**ZU**	**DE**	**DO**
dah	jee	zoo	day	doe
BA	**BI**	**BU**	**BE**	**BO**
bah	bee	boo	bay	boe
PA	**PI**	**PU**	**PE**	**PO**
pah	pee	poo	pay	poe

The *R* sound in Japanese is close to the *L* sound in English, requiring a slight trilling sound to get it right. It resembles the *R* sound in Spanish. Note that the *D* and *Z* sounds are the same in the pronunciations of *ZI* and *JI*.

The following syllables are combinations of some of those appearing above. The two primary syllables are combined into one simply by merging the pronunciations.

RYA r'yah	**RYU** r'yoo	**RYO** r'yoe	(Roll the *R* a bit)
MYA m'yah	**MYU** m'yoo	**MYO** m'yoe	
NYA n'yah	**NYU** n'yoo	**NYO** n'yoe	
HYA h'yah	**HYU** h'yoo	**HYO** h'yoe	
CHA chah	**CHU** choo	**CHO** choe	
SHA shah	**SHU** shoo	**SHO** show	
KYA k'yah	**KYU** cue	**KYO** k'yoe	
PYA p'yah	**PYU** p'yoo	**PYO** p'yoe	
BYA b'yah	**BYU** b'yoo	**BYO** b'yoe	
JA jah	**JU** joo	**JO** joe	
GYA g'yah	**GYU** g'yoo	**GYO** g'yoe	

Keep in mind that the sounds in the chart above are to be pronounced as one syllable, not two. Native English speakers often find *rya* (r'yah), *ryu* (r'yoo), and *ryo* (r'yoe) the hardest to pronounce as one syllable. Try asking a native speaker to say them for you so you can hear how they should sound.

In Japanese, the *H* and *G* sounds are always pronounced as in "how" and "go". There are no true *L* or *V* sounds in Japanese; thus they do not appear in the list of syllables. When the Japanese attempt to pronounce these sounds in English words, the *L* comes out as *R* and the *V* comes out as *B*.

There are long, short, and silent vowels in Japanese, as well as double consonants. The long vowels are designated by a line over them. But you do not have to be overly concerned about long vowels or double consonants when using this book, because the correct pronunciation is generally accounted for in the phonetics.

To get the most out of this guide, first practice pronouncing the syllables—out loud—until you can enunciate each one easily without having to think about it. Before long you will be able to recognize individual syllables in the Japanese words you hear.

Then go to the key-word and key-phrase portion of the book and practice pronouncing the phonetics for each word and sentence, repeating the words and sentences aloud until you can get them out in a smooth flow.

You'll be happy to find that you can communicate in Japanese instantly—simply by reading the phonetic versions of the appropriate words and sentences.

100 KEY WORDS
WITH SAMPLE SENTENCES

PART 1

Words 1–10

1. **ohayō gozaimasu**   (oh-hie-yoe go-zie-mahss)
   good morning

2. **konnichi wa**   (kone-nee-chee wah)
   good afternoon

3. **komban wa**   (kome-bahn wah)
   good evening

4. **dōmo arigatō**   (doe-moe ah-ree-gah-toe)
   thank you very much

5. **sumimasen**   (sue-me-mah-sen)
   pardon me, excuse me

6. **dōzo**   (doe-zoe)
   please
   This is one of the many words that means "please" in

Japanese. *Dōzo* is used only in the sense of "please go first," "please continue," or "after you."

7. kudasai (koo-dah-sie)
please

This word for "please" is almost never used by itself. Rather, it normally follows the command form of verbs as in *tabete kudasai* (tah-bay-tay koo-dah-sie), "please eat," or *nonde kudasai* (noan-day koo-dah-sie), "please drink." It is also used with nouns to convey the meaning of "please ," as in "please bring me water" or "please hand me that."

8. mizu (me-zoo)
water

Please give me (a glass of) water.
Mizu wo* kudasai.
(me-zoo oh koo-dah-sie)

*Wo (oh) is a grammatical particle used to indicate that the preceeding word is the direct object of the action—in this example, water. There are no indefinite or definite articles (a, the) in Japanese, and only a few plural forms.

9. watashi (wah-tah-she)
I

17

There are several commonly used terms in Japanese for the word "I," based on gender and other factors, but *watashi* (wah-tah-she) is standard and can be used by anyone in any situation.

10. **watakushi**   (wah-tock-she)
    I (formal)
    This word for "I" can be used by both men and women in formal as well as informal situations.

• • • • • • • **DEVELOPING VERBAL SKILL** • • • • • • •

It order to develop verbal fluency in Japanese, it is necessary to train the mouth as well as the mind. Simply memorizing words and sentences on a page is obviously not enough. You must be able to say the words or sentences clearly enough that they can be understood.

This means that you must physically train your mouth and tongue to say the foreign words properly—to get them out in a smooth, even flow. In other words, language learning (if you wish to *speak* the language) must be approached as a physical skill, like juggling, playing the guitar, or singing.

For example, pronunciation of the Japanese word *dōitashimashite* (doe-ee-tah-she-mahssh-tay) or "don't mention it," requires seven different tongue and mouth positions. The only way you can master this single word is to say it over and over again, preferably out loud, because this increases confidence in your ability to say it and trains your hearing at the same time.

The key to learning how to speak Japanese is to *speak* it repeatedly— not just read it or read about it—until it comes out automatically, without you having to work too hard.

Kurikaeshi kurikaeshi (koo-ree-kie-eh-she koo-ree-kie-eh-she)—"over and over again"— that is the key to developing great verbal skill.

● ●

PART 2

Words 11–20

11. **watashi ni***   (wah-tah-she nee)

    to me

    *Ni (nee) is a grammatical particle used to indicate that the preceeding word is the indirect object of the action. In this instance *ni* changes "I" to "me," as in "to me" or "for me."

12. **watashi no***   (wah-tah-she no)

    my, mine

    *No (no) is a grammatical particle that changes what precedes it to the possessive case. In this example, adding *no* to *watashi* changes "I" to "my" or "mine."

13. **watashi-tachi / watashi-tachi* no**   (wah-tah-she-tah-chee) / (wah-tah-she-tah-chee no)

    we, us / our, ours

    *Adding *tachi* to personal pronouns makes them plural.

14. desu (dess)

am, is, are

This is a polite word without meaning, but can be thought of as functioning like the verb "to be" in English. Neither *desu* nor any of its forms (see below) are used by themselves. But they are as essential for making correct, complete sentences in Japanese as the English "I am," "you are," "he is," and so forth.

de wa arimasen (day wah ah-ree-mah-sen)

am not, is not, are not

Shortened forms of this include *de wa nai* (day wah nie) and *ja nai* (jah nie).

15. deshita (desh-tah)

was, were

A shortened form of this is *datta*.

de wa arimasen deshita (day wah ah-ree-mah-sen desh-tah)

was not, were not

Shortened forms of this include *de wa nakatta* (day wah nah-kaht-tah) and *ja nakatta* (jah nah-kaht-tah).

16. namae (nah-my)

name

My name is Boye De Mente.
Watashi no namae wa* Boye De Mente desu.
(wah-tah-she no nah-my wah Boye De Mente dess)

*Wa (wah) is a grammatical particle used to indicate that the preceeding word or words are the subject of a sentence. (Another word with the same pronunciation but different Japanese characters means "harmony.")

My name is not Smith.
Watashi no namae wa Sumisu de wa arimasen.
(wah-tah-she no nah-my wah sue-me-sue day wah ah-ree-mah-sen)

17. **nan / nani**   (nahn) / (nah-nee)
    what

18. **anata / anata no**   (ah-nah-tah) / (ah-nah-tah no)
    you / your, yours

What is your name?
Anata no namae wa nan desu ka?*
(ah-nah-tah no nah-my wah nahn dess ka)
*Ka (kah) at the end of a sentence makes it a question.

19. Amerika-jin   (ah-may-ree-kah-jeen)
an American person or people

I am American.
Watashi wa Amerika-jin desu.
(wah-tah-she wah ah-may-ree-kah-jeen dess)

20. Nihon-jin   (nee-hone-jeen)
a Japanese person or people

Are you Japanese?
Anata wa Nihon-jin desu ka?
(ah-nah-tah wah nee-hone-jeen dess kah)

We are British.
Watashi-tachi wa Eikoku-jin desu.
(wah-tah-she-tah-chee wah ay-koe-koo-jeen
dess)

I am Canadian.
Watashi wa Kanada-jin desu.
(wah-tah-she wah kah-nah-dah-jeen dess)

We are Australian.
Watashi-tachi wa Ōsutoraria-jin desu.

(wah-tah-she-tah-chee wah oh-sue-toe-rah-ree-ah-jeen dess)

● ● ● ● ● ● ● ● **DOUBLE CONSONANTS** › ● ● ● ● ● ● ●

Many words in Japanese have double consonants that beginning speakers mispronounce. This can result in language that sounds like gibberish or something entirely different from what is intended. There is an easy way to overcome this problem because Japanese is a language made up of precise syllables.

All you have to do is mentally divide the sounds of such words into their phonetic equivalents (as all Japanese words are in this book), and account for the double consonant sounds by incorporating them into the phonetic syllables. Try pronouncing the following examples:

> **kekko**   (keck-koe)
> fine, alright
> **matte kudasai**   (maht-tay koo-dah-sie)
> please wait
> **itte kudasai**   (eat-tay koo-dah-sie)
> please go
> **tomatte kudasai**   (toe-maht-tay koo-dah-sie)
> please stop
> **haitte kudasai**   (hite-tay koo-dah-sie)
> please come in

gakkō　(gahk-koe)
school
yukkuri　(yuke-koo-ree)
slow

To pronounce these words, just say each of the individual phonetic syllables fully and clearly. You will hear a very slight pause before the double consonants, similar to the sound in the English word "bookkeeper."

● ●

PART 3

Words 21–30

21. donata / donata no   (doe-nah-tah) / (doe-nah-tah no)
who / whose

Who are you?
Anata wa donata desu ka?
(ah-nah-tah wah doe-nah-tah dess kah)

22. kore   (koe-ray)
this

Whose is this?
Kore wa donata no desu ka?
(koe-ray wah doe-nah-tah no dess kah)

It is mine.
Watashi no desu.   ("it" is understood)
(wah-tah-she no dess)

It is ours.
Watashi-tachi no desu.
(wah-tah-she-tah-chee no dess)

23. **sore** (soe-ray)
    that

    What is that?
    Sore wa nan desu ka?
    (soe-ray wah nahn dess kah)

    Whose is that?
    Sore wa donata no desu ka?
    (soe-ray wah doe-nah-tah no dess kah)

    Is that yours?
    Sore wa anata no desu ka?
    (soe-ray wah ah-nah-tah no dess kah)

24. **ano hito / ano hito no** (ah-no ssh-toe) / (ah-
    no ssh-toe no)
    he, she, him, her / his, hers

    That is hers.
    Sore wa ano hito no desu.
    (soe-ray wah ah-no ssh-toe no dess)

Who is that?
Ano hito wa donata desu ka?
(ah-no ssh-toe wah doe-nah-tah dess kah)

What is his name?
Ano hito no namae wa nan desu ka?
(ah-no ssh-toe no nah-my wah nahn dess kah)

His name is Green.
Guriin desu. ("his name" is understood)
(goo-reen dess)

25. **messēji**   (may-say-jee)
    message

    Do you have a message for me?
    Watashi ni messēji ga* arimasu ka?
    (wah-tah-she nee may-say-jee gah ah-ree-mahss kah)

    *Ga (gah) is similar to wa but often signals new
    information being introduced—a new message as
    opposed to the (previously known) message.

26. **itsu**   (eat-sue)
    when

When is it?
Itsu desu ka?
(eat-sue dess kah)

27. **doko**   (doe-koe)
    where

    Where is it?
    Doko desu ka?
    (doe-koe dess kah)

    Where is the bathroom (toilet/washroom)?*
    O-tearai wa doko desu ka?
    (oh-tay-ah-rie wah doe-koe dess kah)

    *There are specific words for bathroom and toilet, but
    the most common general term is *o-tearai* . Literally it
    means "hand wash."

28. **hai**   (hi)
    yes

29. **sō desu**   (soh dess)
    yes, that's so, that's right
    This affirmative expression is commonly used for "yes"
    and is more polite than the term *hai*.

30. iie   (eee-eh)
no

No, that is not correct.
Iie, sō de wa arimasen.
(eee-eh soh day wah ah-ree-mah-sen)

The word "no" is not used as much in Japanese as it is in English. The preferred way of expressing "no" is to use the negative form of the key verb. For example, *iku?* (ee-koo) meaning "are you going?" is generally answered with *ikanai* (ee-kah-nie), "I'm not going," rather than *iie* (eee-eh), a blunt "no."

• • • • • •   **PRONOUNCING JAPANESE**   • • • • • •

Anyone familiar with the pronunciation of Latin, Italian, Spanish, Portugese, or Hawaiian, has a head start in learning how to pronounce Japanese correctly. In fact, when the sounds of the Japanese language are transcribed into Roman letters (the familiar ABC's), they are pronounced virtually the same as in these languages.

The key to pronouncing Japanese properly is found in the vowels: *a, i, u, e* and *o*. In Japanese the *a* is pronounced as *ah*, the *i* as *ee*, the *u* as *oo*, the *e* as *eh*, the *o* as *oh*—just as in the above languages. For example, Narita (nah-ree-tah), the name of Tōkyō's international airport, would be pronounced exactly the same in Spanish, and vice-versa. The Spanish word *casa* is pronounced the same in both languages, as is *mesa*, *cara*, *rio*, *Maria*, and so on.

One significant difference between the pronunciation of Spanish and Japanese words is found in the *L* and *V* sounds. There is no true *L* or *V* sound in Japanese. The *L* comes out as an *R* sound and the *V* as a *B* sound. So "Lolita" in Japanese is *Rorita*; "via" becomes *bia*, etc.

● ●

PART 4
Words 31–40

31. iku   (ee-koo)
to go

Japanese verbs are regularly used alone in their present, past, and future tenses as well as in their negative and interrogative forms, as complete sentences. The rest of the meaning is understood from the context. Japanese verb endings do not change when the subjects change as they do in English. Therefore *ikimasu* (ee-kee-mahss) can mean "I go," "you go," "he goes," "she goes," "it goes," "we go" or "they go." In the following example sentences only one subject is translated into English for simplicity, but don't forget that a variety of subjects is possible.

Ikimasu.   (ee-kee-mahss)
I am going. I will go.
Ikimasen.   (ee-kee-mah-sen)
I am not going. I will not go.
The abbreviated form is *ikanai* (ee-kah-nie).

Ikimasu ka?   (ee-kee-mahss kah)
Are you going?
Ikimashita.   (ee-kee-mahssh-tah)
I went.
Ikitai.   (ee-kee-tie)
I want to go.
Ikimashō.   (ee-kee-mah-show)
Let's go.
Itte kudasai.   (eat-tay koo-dah-sie)
Please go.

Where are you going?
Doko ni ikimasu ka?
(doe-koe nee ee-kee-mahss kah)

Where is he going?
Ano hito wa doko ni ikimasu ka?
(ah-no ssh-toe wah doe-koe nee ee-kee-mahss
kah)

Where do you want to go?
Doko ni ikitai desu ka?
(doe-koe nee ee-kee-tie dess kah)

32. **hoteru**   (hoe-tay-rue)
    hotel

33

I want to go to my hotel.
Hoteru ni ikitai desu.
(hoe-tay-rue nee ee-kee-tie dess)

I want to go to the New Otani Hotel.
Nyū Ōtani Hoteru ni ikitai desu.
(new oh-tah-nee hoe-tay-rue nee ee-kee-tie dess)

My hotel is the Ginza Atamiso.
Watashi no hoteru wa Ginza no Atamisō desu.
(wah-tah-she no hoe-tay-rue wah geen-zah no
ah-tah-me-soh dess)

33. **taberu**   (tah-bay-rue)
    to eat

    Tabemasu.   (tah-bay-mahss)
    I eat (it). I will eat. I am ready to eat.
    Tabemasu ka?   (tah-bay-mahss kah)
    Will you eat (it)? Do you eat (that)?
    Tabemasen.   (tah-bay-mah-sen)
    I am not going to eat. I do not eat (that).
    Tabemashita.   (tah-bay-mahssh-tah)
    I ate.
    Tabetai.   (tah-bay-tie)
    I want to eat.

Tabemashō. (tah-bay-mah-show)
Let's eat.
Tabete kudasai. (tah-bay-tay koo-dah-sie)
Please eat.

Where are we going to eat?
Doko de tabemasu ka?
(doe-koe day tah-bay-mahss kah)

Where do you want to eat?
Doko de tabetai desu ka?
(doe-koe day tah-bay-tie dess kah)

What do you want to eat?
Nani wo tabetai desu ka?
(nah-nee oh tah-bay-tie dess kah)

34. **shokuji** (show-koo-jee)
food

Let's eat (some food).
(Shokuji wo) tabemashō.
(show-koo-jee oh tah-bay-mah-show)

35. **washoku** (wah-show-koo)
Japanese food

35

I want to eat Japanese food.
Washoku wo* tabetai desu.
(wa-show-koo oh tah-bay-tie dess)

*As mentioned earlier, *wo* (oh) is a grammatical particle used to indicate that the preceeding word is the direct object of the sentence.

36. **yōshoku**　(yoh-show-koo)
Western food

Let's eat Western food.
Yōshoku wo tabemashō.
(yoh-show-koo oh tah-bay-mah-show)

Where shall we eat?
Doko de tabemashō ka?
(doe-koe day tah-bay-mah-show kah)

Have you already eaten?
Mō tabemashita ka?
(moe tah-bay-mahssh-tah kah)

I don't want to eat.
Tabetaku nai.
(tah-bay-tah-koo nie)

I don't want to eat Western food.
Yōshoku wo tabetaku nai desu.
(yoe-show-koo oh tah-bay-tah-koo nie dess)

37. nomu   (no-moo)
to drink

Nomimasu.   (no-me-mahss)
I drink. I will drink.
Nomimasen.   (no-me-mah-sen)
I do not drink. I will not drink.
This is also used for "I don't want anything to drink."
Nomimasu ka?   (no-me-mahss ka)
Will you (have a) drink?
Nomimashita.   (no-me-mahssh-tah)
I drank (already).
Nomitai.   (no-me-tie)
I want to drink.
Nomimashō.   (no-me-mah-show)
Let's drink.
Nonde kudasai.   (noan-day koo-dah-sie)
Please drink.
Nomanai de kudasai.   (no-mah-nie day koo-dah-sie)
Please don't drink.

Would you like something to drink?
Nani ka* nomitai desu ka?
(nah-nee kah no-me-tie dess kah)

*Putting *ka* after *nani* changes the meaning from "what" to "something."

I'd like to drink a cola.
Kōra wo nomitai.
(koe-rah oh no-me-tie)

I'd like a beer.
Biiru wo nomitai.
(bee-rue oh no-me-tie)

I do not drink *sake*.
Sake wo nomimasen.
(sah-kay oh no-me-mah-sen)

38. suki (ski)
like (be fond of, love)

Do you like sushi?
Sushi ga suki desu ka?
(sue-she gah ski dess kah)

I don't like it.

Suki de wa arimasen.
(ski de wah ah-ree-mah-sen)

I want (would like) to eat sushi.
Sushi wo tabetai desu.
(sue-she oh tah-bay-tie dess)

I don't like that.
Sore ga suki de wa arimasen.
(soe-ray gah ski day wah ah-ree-mah-sen)

I like this.
Kore ga suki desu.
(koe-ray gah ski dess)

I don't like this.
Kore ga suki de wa arimasen.
(koe-ray gah ski day wah ah-ree-mah-sen)

I don't like whiskey.
Uisukii ga suki de wa arimasen.
(oo-iss-key gah ski day wah ah-ree-mah-sen)

39. **itadakimasu**   (ee-tah-dah-kee-mahss)
    to receive, accept
    This expression is regularly said just before beginning

a meal (particularly when you are a guest). The literal meaning is "I receive/accept (this food)." In general this is a formal, polite way of expressing appreciation and thanks. Prior to taking the first drink, the traditional Japanese salutation is *kampai!* (kahm-pie).

40. oishii   (oh-ee-she-e)
(it is) delicious

oishikatta   (oh-ee-she-kaht-tah)
(it was) delicious

Is it good?
Oishii desu ka?
(oh-ee-she-e dess kah)

• • • • • • • •   **WRITING JAPANESE**   • • • • • • • •

There are four different ways of writing the Japanese language—although one of them is generally limited to foreign words written phonetically so they can be pronounced easily. These four ways are:

1. *Kanji* (kahn-jee) or ideograms (originally imported from China), which are used together with a phonetic script called *hiragana* (he-rah-gah-nah). This is the standard and most common way of writing Japanese.

40

2. *Hiragana*, the phonetic script which is used together with *kanji* for verb endings, prepositions, etc. In texts written for children it is common to use only *hiragana* because that is what they first learn to read.

3. *Katakana* (kah-tah-kah-nah), another phonetic script which is primarily reserved for transcribing foreign words into Japanese syllables. For example, the Japanese word for "computer," which is *kompyūtā* (komep'yoo-tah), is always written in *katakana* script.

4. *Rōmaji* (roe-mah-jee), or "Roman letters," which was originally used by and for the benefit of foreigners who could not read *kanji* or *hiragana*. It is now commonly used on signs all over Japan—usually in conjunction with *kanji, hiragana* , or both.

The reading and writing of romanized Japanese *(rōmaji)* is not taught as a regular course in public schools, so only those who study privately develop skill in reading it. *Rōmaji* is, however, commonly used on a variety of school materials, advertising, shop signs and so on, though sometimes, it seems, just for exotic effect.

●●●●●●●●●●●●●●●●●●●●●●●●●●●●

PART 5

Words 41–50

41. gochisōsama deshita (go-chee-soh-sah-mah desh-tah)

Thank you for the meal.

This is a formal and common way of expressing thanks and appreciation to the person who has prepared or paid for a meal.

42. au (ah-oo)

to meet

Remember that subjects are often unexpressed in Japanese. The following sentences are translated into English using the subject "I," but could also be understood to mean "he," "she," "they," "we," "it," "that person," and so forth.

Aimasu. (eye-mahss)
I will meet (someone).
Aimasen. (eye-mah-sen)
I will not meet (someone).

Aimasu ka?   (eye-mahss kah)
Will you meet me?
Aimashita.   (eye-mahssh-tah)
I met (someone).
Aitai.   (eye-tie)
I want to meet (you).
Aimashō.   (eye-mah-show)
Let's meet.

Where shall we meet?
Doko de aimashō ka?
(doe-koe day eye-mah-show kah)

Please meet me at the hotel.
Hoteru de *aimashō.
(hoe-tay-rue day eye-mah-show)
*The word preceeding the particle *de* (day) often
indicates a place where the action of the verb will
happen.

Please meet me in the lobby.
Robii de aimashō.
(roe-bee day eye-mah-show)

43. **nanji**   (nahn-jee)
what time

What time shall we meet?
Nanji ni aimashō ka?
(nahn-jee nee eye-mah-show kah)

Where shall we meet tonight?
Komban doko de aimashō ka?
(kome-bahn doe-koe day eye-mah-show kah)

What time do you want to go?
Nanji ni ikitai desu ka?
(nahn-jee nee ee-kee-tie dess kah)

What time are we going to eat?
Nanji ni tabemasu ka?
(nahn-jee nee tah-bay-mahss kah)

When shall we meet?
Itsu aimashō ka?
(eat-sue eye-mah-show kah)

44. **aru** (ah-rue)
to be, have (for objects)

Arimasu. (ah-ree-mahss)
There is. There are. I have.
Arimasen. (ah-ree-mah-sen)

There is not. There are not. I do not have.
Arimasu ka?   (ah-ree-mahss kah)
Is there any? Do you have some?
Arimashita.   (ah-ree-mahssh-tah)
There was. There were. I had.

Do you have some (any/it)? Is there any?
Arimasu ka?
(ah-ree-mahss kah)

No, I don't have any (it). There is none.
Arimasen.
(ah-ree-mah-sen)

45. **ikura**   (ee-koo-rah)
      how much

How much is this?
Kore wa ikura desu ka?
(koe-ray wah ee-koo-rah dess kah)

How much is that?
Sore wa ikura desu ka?
(soe-ray wah ee-koo-rah dess kah)

How much is it?

Ikura desu ka?
(ee-koo-rah dess kah)

46. **takai**   (tah-kie)
high, expensive

That is expensive.
Sore wa takai desu.
(soe-ray wah tah-kie dess)

47. **yasui**   (yah-sue-e)
cheap, inexpensive

Do you have a cheap one?
Yasui no wa arimasu ka?
(yah-sue-e no wah ah-ree-mahss kah)

48. **suru**   (sue-rue)
to do

Shimasu.   (she-mahss)
I do (it). I will do. I am going to do.
Shimasen.   (she-mah-sen)
I do not do (it). I will not do. I am not going to do.
Shimasu ka?   (she-mahssh-kah)

Do you do (it)? Will you do?
Shimashita.   (she-mahssh-tah)
I did (it).
Shitai.   (she-tie)
I want to do (it).
Shimashō.   (she-mah-show)
Let's do (it).
Shite kudasai.   (ssh-tay koo-dah-sie)
Please do (it).
Shinai de kudasai.   (she-nie day koo-dah-sie)
Please don't do (it).

What shall we do?
Nani wo shimashō ka?
(nah-nee oh she-mah-show kah)

What are you doing?
Nani wo shite imasu* ka?
(nah-nee oh ssh-tay ee-mahss kah)
*Shite imasu (ssh-tay ee-mahss) is the present progressive form of *shimasu*, which changes "do" into "doing."

What are you (we) going to do?
Dō* shimasu ka?
(doh she-mahss kah)

47

How should it be done? / How should I do it?
Dō* iu fū ni shimasu ka?
(doh yoo fuu nee she-mahss kah)
*Dō (doh) can mean "what," "how," or "why,"
depending on the usage.

What is he doing?
Ano hito wa nani wo shite imasu ka?
(ah-no ssh-toe wah nah-nee oh ssh-tay ee-mahss
kah)

What do you want to do?
Nani wo shitai desu ka?
(nah-nee oh she-tie dess kah)

I don't want to do anything.
Nani mo shitaku nai.
(nah-nee moe she-tah-koo nie)

What did you do?
Nani wo shimashita ka?
(nah-nee oh she-mahssh-tah kah)

I didn't do anything.
Nani mo shimasen deshita.
(nah-nee moe she-mah-sen desh-tah)

49. ii   (eee)
good (fine, acceptable)

Is it OK?
Ii desu ka?
(eee dess kah)

Is this OK?
Kore wa ii desu ka?
(koe-ray wah eee dess kah)

That's fine.
Sore wa ii desu.
(soe-ray wah eee dess)

Is it OK to go?
Itte* mo ii desu ka?
(eat-tay moe eee dess kah)

*Itte (eat-tay) is a form of *ikimasu* (go) that by itself is a command, as in *itte kudasai* (eat-tay koo-dah-sie), "please go." *Mo ii desu ka?* after a verb adds the sense of "may I . . . ?" or "is it alright to . . . ?"

Is it OK to eat?
Tabete mo ii desu ka?
(tah-bay-tay moe eee dess kah)

Is it OK to do it?
Shite mo ii desu ka?
(ssh-tay moe eee dess kah)

What time are we (you) going?
Nanji ni ikimasu ka?
(nahn-jee nee ee-kee-mahss kah)

50. **dochira** (doe-chee-rah)
which (of two)
dore (doe-ray)
which (of many)

Which one is yours?
Dochira ga anata no desu ka?
(doe-chee-rah gah ah-nah-tah no dess kah)

Which one is good (the best)?
Dore ga ii desu ka?
(doe-ray gah eee dess kah)

Which one is (the most) expensive?
Dochira ga takai desu ka?
(doe-chee-rah gah tah-kie dess kah)

• • • • • WRITING JAPANESE IN "ENGLISH" • • • • •

The earliest Western visitors to Japan faced an enormous challenge in trying to learn the Japanese language because it was written in a script they could not pronounce. Several of the more scholarly inclined of these early visitors created phonetic systems based on the familiar ABC's for writing the language. Unfortunately, each of these systems was designed for speakers of a specific language (Portuguese, Dutch, German, English), and was therefore not universally practical for all foreigners wanting to learn Japanese.

Finally, an American medical missionary named Dr. James Curtis Hepburn, who went to Japan in 1859 after earlier spending fourteen years in Singapore and Amoy, collaborated in the development of a romanizing system *(rōmaji)* based on English that was eventually to become the standard. This is known as the "Hepburn System."

While in Japan, Dr. Hepburn helped found Meiji Gakuen University and served as its first president. His publication in 1867 of *A Japanese-English Dictionary*, the first such dictionary, played a key role in introducing Japan to the outside world. Dr. Hepburn returned to the U.S. in 1892 and died in 1911.

Some Japanese educators and scholars did not appreciate the fact that a foreigner had played a leading role in the development of *rōmaji,* and came up with a number of systems based on Japanese perspectives. But these systems did not win popular support. The Hepburn System, officially referred to as the *hyōjun* (h'yoe-june) or "standard" system, is used in Japan by most government and private institutions, and almost exclusively outside of Japan.

The main reason that the Japanese romanizing systems have not succeeded in competing with or replacing the Hepburn system is because they make use of Chinese-style romanization in which several sounds are represented by letters that are quite different from their use in English and the Romance languages of Europe. For example, *ti* stands for the sound *chi, tu* for the sound *tsu, z* for *j,* and so on.

● ●

PART 6

Words 51–60

51. chiisai   (chee-e-sie)
small, little

I like the small one.
Chiisai no wa suki desu.
(chee-e-sie no wah ski dess)

Which one is small (the smallest)?
Dochira ga chiisai desu ka?
(doe-chee-rah gah chee-e-sie dess kah)

This is too small.
Kore wa chiisa sugimasu.
(koe-ray wah chee-e-sah sue-ghee-mahss)

I will take the small one.
Chiisai no wo itadakimasu.
(chee-e-sie no oh ee-tah-dah-kee-mahss)

52. ōkii   (oh-kee-e)
large, big

Do you have a bigger one?
Motto* ōkii no wa arimasu ka?
(mote-toe oh-kee-e no wah ah-ree-mahss kah)
*_Motto_ adds the meaning of more; in this example it is "more big," meaning "larger" or "bigger."

Do you have a smaller one?
Motto chiisai no wa arimasu ka?
(mote-toe chee-e-sie no wah ah-ree-mahss kah)

53. ichiban*   (ee-chee-bahn)
number one
*When used before adjectives, _ichiban_ forms the superlative (-est) form.

Which one is the cheapest?
Dochira ga ichiban yasui desu ka?
(doe-chee-rah gah ee-chee-bahn yah-sue-ee dess kah)

Which one is the best?
Dore ga ichiban ii desu ka?
(doe-ray gah ee-chee-bahn eee dess kah)

Which one do you like?
Dore ga suki desu ka?
(doe-ray gah ski dess kah)

I will take that one. How much is it?
Sore wo itadakimasu. Ikura desu ka?
(soe-ray oh ee-tah-dah-kee-mahss, ee-koo-rah
dess kah)

54. **dasu**   (dah-sue)
to send, mail

   Dashimasu.   (dah-she-mahss)
   I will mail (it).
   Dashimasen.   (dah-she-mah-sen)
   I did not send (it). I will not send (it).
   Dashimashita.   (dah-she-mahssh-tah)
   I sent (it).
   Dashitai.   (dah-ssh-tie)
   I want to mail (this).
   Dashite kudasai.   (dah-ssh-tay koo-dah-sie)
   Please send (this). Please mail (it).

   Please mail this today.
   Kore wo kyō dashite kudasai.
   (koe-ray oh k'yoe dah-ssh-tay koo-dah-sie)

55. koko   (koe-koe)
here

Let's have something to drink here.
Koko de nani ka nomimashō.
(koe-koe day nah-nee kah no-me-mah-show)

Where is this?
Koko wa doko desu ka?
(koe-koe wah doe-koe dess kah)

Is this place OK?
Koko wa ii desu ka?
(koe-koe wah eee dess kah)

56. tomaru   (toe-mah-rue)
to stop (come to rest)

Tomarimasu.   (toe-mah-ree-mahss)
I stop. I will stop.
Tomarimasen.   (toe-mah-ree-mah-sen)
I do not stop. I will not stop.
Tomarimashita.   (toe-mah-ree-mahssh-tah)
I stopped.
Tomarimasu ka?   (toe-mah-ree-mahssh kah)
Do you stop? Will you stop?

Tomaritai.   (toe-mah-ree-tie)
I want to stop.
Tomarimashō.   (toe-mah-ree-mah-show)
Let's stop.
Tomatte kudasai.   (toe-maht-tay koo-dah-sie)
Please stop.

Please stop here.
Koko de tomatte kudasai.
(koe-koe day toe-maht-tay koo-dah-sie)

I want to stop here.
Koko de tomaritai desu.
(koe-koe day toe-mah-ree-tie dess)

Where shall we stop?
Doko de tomarimashō ka?
(doe-koe day toe-mah-ree-mah-show kah)

Where are we stopping tonight?
Komban* doko de tomarimasu ka?
(kome-bahn doe-koe day toe-mah-ree-mahss
kah)

*Komban (tonight) is the same komban that you saw
earlier in komban wa, which means "good evening."
You can use komban wa as soon as it's dark.

57. matsu   (maht-sue)
to wait

Machimasu.   (mah-chee-mahss)
I will wait.
Machimasen.   (mah-chee-mah-sen)
I will not wait.
Machimasu ka?   (mah-chee-mahss kah)
Will you wait?
Machimashita.   (mah-chee-mahssh-tah)
I waited.
Machitai.   (mah-chee-tie)
I want to wait.
Machimashō   (mah-chee-mah-show)
Let's wait.
Matte kudasai.   (maht-tay koo-dah-sie)
Please wait.

I will wait for you here.
Koko de machimasu.
(koe-koe day mah-chee-mahss)

Wait here.
Koko de matte kudasai.
(koe-koe day maht-tay koo-dah-sie)

I will wait at the hotel.
Hoteru de machimasu.
(hoe-tay-rue day mah-chee-mahss)

I will wait in my room.
Rūmu de machimasu.
(rue-moo day mah-chee-mahss)

Is it OK if I wait here?
Koko de matte mo ii desu ka?
(koe-koe day maht-tay moe eee dess kah)

Please don't wait.
Matanai de kudasai.
(mah-tah-nie day koo-dah-sie)

58. **kuru**   (koo-rue)
     to come

> **Kimasu.**   (kee-mahss)
> I will come.
> **Kimasen.**   (kee-mah-sen)
> I will not come.
> **Kimasu ka?**   (kee-mahss kah)
> Will you come?

Kimashita.   (kee-mahssh-tah)
I came.
Kite kudasai.   (kee-tay koo-dah-sie)
Please come.

Is he coming here? Are you coming here?
Koko ni kimasu ka?
(koe-koe nee kee-mahss kah)

Is she coming this afternoon? Are you coming
this afternoon?
Kyō no gogo ni kimasu ka?
(k'yoe no go-go nee kee-mahss kah)

I am not coming. They are not coming. She is
not coming.
Kimasen.
(kee-mah-sen)

59. **kau**   (kah-oo)
    to buy

    Kaimasu.   (kie-mahss)
    I will buy (it).
    Kaimasen.   (kie-mah-sen)
    I will not buy (it).

Kaimasu ka?   (kie-mahss kah)
Will you buy (it)? Are you going to buy (it)?
Kaimashita.   (kie-mahssh-tah)
I bought (it).
Kaitai.   (kie-tie)
I want to buy (this).
Kaimashō.   (kie-mah-show)
Let's buy (it).
Katte kudasai.   (kaht-tay koo-dah-sie)
Please buy (it).

I want to buy that.
Sore wo kaitai desu.
(sore-ray oh kie-tie dess)

What do you want to buy?
Nani wo kaitai desu ka?
(nah-nee oh kie-tie dess kah)

Please buy it for me.
Watashi ni katte kudasai.
(wah-tah-shee nee kaht-tay koo-dah-sie)

Where did you buy that?
Sore wo doko de kaimashita ka?
(soe-ray oh doe-koe day kie-mahssh-tah kah)

Did you buy this at a department store?
Kore wo depāto de kaimashita ka?
(koe-ray oh day-pah-to day kie-mahssh-tah kah)

What did you buy?
Nani wo kaimashita ka?
(nah-nee oh kie-mahssh-tah kah)

60. **kaimono** (kie-moe-no)
shopping

I want to go shopping.
Kaimono ni ikitai desu.
(kie-moe-no nee ee-kee-tie dess)

Let's go shopping.
Kaimono ni ikimashō.
(kie-moe-no nee ee-kee-mah-show)

Did you go shopping?
Kaimono ni ikimashita ka?
(kie-moe-no nee ee-kee-mahssh-tah kah)

I like shopping!
Kaimono ga suki desu!
(kie-moe-no gah ski dess)

• • • • DEALING WITH JAPANIZED ENGLISH • • • •

Some 20,000 foreign words, mostly from English, have been merged into the Japanese language, and are now as commonly used as native Japanese terms. But this massive adoption of English vocabulary has not made it much easier for non-Japanese speaking people to understand or learn the language.

The reason for this rather odd problem is that all of the adopted English words are written and pronounced according to Japanese pronunciation. That is, each word is broken up into Japanese syllables which are then written or pronounced in the normal Japanese way.

This means that a simple English word like "strike" becomes *sutoraiki* (sue-toe-rye-kee), "milk" becomes *miruku* (me-rue-koo), "blue" becomes *burū* (boo-rue), "sex" becomes *sekusu* (say-koo-sue)—all of which are absolutely meaningless to a native English speaker until the meanings of the words are explained—or unless the foreigner is familiar enough with this Japanization process to convert it back to English automatically.

Other foreign words are abbreviated as they are Japanized, making them even harder to understand. A recent news issue is that of *sekuhara,* which means "sexual harassment" and was created by combining the first parts of the two English words.

When Japanized English words are used by themselves, or in abbreviated contexts in which the meaning is not obvious, they are like any other foreign language that one has to learn in order to understand.

My daughter Demetra, who spent six months in Tōkyō studying Japanese, went shopping one day and was stumped for hours by the term *berubetto* (bay-rue-bait-toe). A bi-lingual girlfriend solved the mystery for her—velvet.

● ●

PART 7
Words 61–70

61. o-kane (oh-kah-nay)
money

Is this your money?
Kore wa anata no o-kane desu ka?
(koe-ray wah ah-nah-tah no oh-kah-nay dess
kah)

Yes, it is.
Hai, sō desu.
(hi, soh dess)

62. motsu (moat-sue)
to have

Motte imasu. (moat-tay e-mahss)
I have.
Motte imasen. (moat-tay e-mah-sen)

I do not have.

Do you have any Japanese money?
Nihon no o-kane wo motte imasu ka?
(nee-hone no oh-kah-nay oh moat-tay e-mahss
kah)

No, I don't.
Motte imasen.
(moat-tay e-mah-sen)

Do you have any dollars?
Doru wo motte imasu ka?
(doe-rue oh moat-tay ee-mahss kah)

Yes, I have.
Motte imasu.
(moat-tay ee-mahss)

What do you have?
Nani wo motte imasu ka?
(nah-nee oh mote-tay ee-mahss kah)

63. yobu   (yoe-boo)
     to call (out to someone, call a taxi, etc.)

Yobimasu.   (yoe-bee-mahss)
I call (someone).
Yobimasen.   (yoe-bee-mah-sen)
I do not call.
Yobimasu ka?   (yoe-bee-mahss kah)
Will you call?
Yobimashita.   (yoe-bee-mahssh-tah)
I called.
Yobimashō.   (yoe-bee-mah-show)
Let's call (someone).
Yonde kudasai.   (yoan-day koo-dah-sie)
Please call (someone).

Did you call me?
Yobimashita ka?
(yoe-bee-mahssh-tah ka)

Who called me?
Donata ga watashi wo yobimashita ka?
(doe-nah-tah gah wah-tah-she oh yoe-bee-
mahssh-tah kah)

Please call him.
Ano hito wo yonde kudasai.
(ah-no ssh-toe oh yoan-day koo-dah-sie)

64. denwa wo suru   (den-wah oh sue-rue)
to telephone

Denwa wo shimasu.   (den-wah oh she-
mahss)
I telephone.
Denwa wo shimasen.   (den-wah oh she-mah-
sen)
I will not telephone.
Denwa wo shimashita.   (den-wah oh she-
mahssh-tah)
I telephoned.
Denwa wo shitai.   (den-wah oh she-tie)
I want to telephone.
Denwa wo shimashō.   (den-wah oh she-mah-
show)
Let's telephone.

Was there a telephone call (for me)?
Denwa ga arimashita ka?
(den-wah gah ah-ree-mahssh-tah kah)

Please telephone me.
Denwa wo shite kudasai.
(den-wah oh ssh-tay koo-dah-sie)

Please telephone him (her).
Ano hito ni denwa wo shite kudasai.
(ah-no ssh-toe nee den-wah oh ssh-tay koo-dah-sie)

Please telephone my hotel.
Watashi no hoteru ni denwa wo shite kudasai.
(wah-tah-she no hoe-tay-rue nee den-wah oh ssh-tay koo-dah-sie)

Mr. Smith, telephone (for you).
Sumisu-san, denwa desu.
(sue-me-sue-sahn, den-wah dess)

Who is the telephone call for?
Denwa wa donata ni desu ka?
(den-wah wah doe-nah-tah nee dess kah)

I will call you.
Denwa shimasu.
(den-wah she-mahss)

I called you.
Denwa shimashita.
(den-wah she-mahssh-tah)

65. kaku   (kah-koo)
   to write

   Kakimasu.   (kah-kee-mahss)
   I write.
   Kakimasen.   (kah-kee-mah-sen)
   I will not write.
   Kakimasu ka?   (kah-kee-mahss kah)
   Will you write?
   Kakimashita.   (kah-kee-mahssh-tah)
   I wrote.
   Kakitai.   (kah-kee-tie)
   I want to write.

   Please sign your name here.
   Koko ni namae wo kaite kudasai.
   (koe-koe nee nah-my oh kie-tay koo-dah-sie)

   Where do I sign my name?
   Namae wo doko de kakimasu ka?
   (nah-my oh doe-koe day kah-kee-mahss kah)

   It is written down.
   Kaite arimasu.
   (kie-tay ah-ree-mahss)

Please write it down.
Kaite kudasai.
(kie-tay koo-dah-sie)

66. **dekiru**   (day-kee-rue)
able to do, can do

Dekimasu.   (day-kee-mahss)
I can do (it).
Dekimasen.   (day-kee-mah-sen)
I cannot do (it).
Dekimasu ka?   (day-kee-mahss kah)
Can you do (it)?
Dekimashita.   (day-kee-mahssh-tah)
I did (it).

Can you do something (about it)?
Nani ka dekimasu ka?
(nah-nee kah day-kee-mahss ka)

Can you do it?
Dekimasu ka?
(day-kee-mahss kah)

I cannot do it.

71

Dekimasen.
(day-kee-mah-sen)

I cannot do anything (about it).
Nani mo dekimasen.
(nah-nee moe day-kee-mah-sen)

67. **kyō**   (k'yoe)
today

Can you do it today?
Kyō dekimasu ka?
(k'yoe day-kee-mahss kah)

Where are you (we, they) going today?
Kyō doko ni ikimasu ka?
(k'yoe doe-koe nee ee-kee-mahss kah)

Today I'm (we're, they're) not going anywhere at all.
Kyō doko ni mo ikimasen.
(k'yoe doe-koe nee moe ee-kee-mah-sen)

68. **ashita**   (ahssh-tah)
tomorrow

Can you do it by tomorrow?
Ashita made ni* dekimasu ka?
(ahssh-tah mah-day nee day-kee-mahss kah)
*Made (mah-day) means "until" and made ni (mah-day nee) means "by."

Where would you like to go tomorrow?
Ashita doko ni ikitai desu ka?
(ahssh-tah doe-koe nee ee-kee-tie dess kah)

69. **Eigo**   (a-e-go)
English
Pronounce the ei of eigo like "ay" in "hay."

Can you speak English? (literally: "do" English)
Eigo ga dekimasu ka?
(a-e-go gah day-kee-mahss kah)

70. **Nihongo**   (nee-hone-go)
Japanese

I cannot speak Japanese. (literally: "do" Japanese)
Nihongo ga dekimasen.
(nee-hone-go gah day-kee-mah-sen)

• • • • LEVELS OF POLITENESS IN JAPANESE • • • •

Japanese, like a number of other languages, has more than one level of polite speech that involves vocabulary, word endings, and even a change in physical posture. These levels are referred to as *keigo* (kay-e-go), which is generally translated as "polite speech" or "honorifics," in reference to "high level" Japanese. Humble Japanese, which you use when referring to yourself, is also a kind of *keigo*.

On the ultra-polite level, "to be" (*desu*) becomes *de gozaimasu* (day go-zie-mahss). There are many other extremely polite forms and words. For example, there are three different words for "say": the humble *mōsu* (moe-sue), the standard *iu* (yoo), and the ultra-polite *ossharu* (oh-shah-rue).

Adding *o-* to the front of nouns and some adjectives and adverbs makes them (and your speech) extra polite. Japan's famous rice wine, *sake* (sah-kay) is often called *o-sake* (oh-sah-kay).

Japan's different levels of speech developed because of a feudal social system in which rank was expressed by both speech forms and rituals, including kneeling or sitting on the floor and bowing. The level of speech that was appropriate in any situation was determined by the social positions of the people involved. Age and gender were also key elements.

The physical etiquette and manner of speaking developed by the ruling samurai class was so precise and comprehensive that it took years to learn and required constant attention to perform properly. Failure to speak in an accepted manner to a superior was a very serious offense. In some cases it could result in the death penalty.

Women, especially older women, will normally use a higher level of speech than men even in ordinary circumstances. In informal situations, men (except those who are highly cultured) commonly use a rougher, coarser level of Japanese that sounds like a dialect to untutored ears. A number of Japan's traditional professions, including that of the *yakuza* (yah-koo-zah) gangsters, have their own language with distinctive vocabulary and ways of speaking.

The ubiquitous *san* (sahn) that is attached to the end of names is the equivalent of Mr., Mrs., or Miss. It is very important to use *san* even in situations calling for ordinary, polite speech because not using it may be considered rude, insulting, arrogant, or worse. However, you should note that honorific prefixes and words are generally not used when referring to oneself or one's family members. For example, you should never introduce yourself as So & So-*san*.

● ●

PART 8

Words 71–80

71. ikutsu   (ee-koot-sue)
how many

How many do you have (are there)?
Ikutsu arimasu ka?
(ee-koot-sue ah-ree-mahss kah)

72. iru   (ee-rue)
to need, want

Irimasu.   (ee-ree-mahss)
I need (something).
Irimasen.   (ee-ree-mah-sen)
I don't need (it).
Irimasu ka?   (ee-ree-mahss kah)
Do you need (it)?
Irimashita.   (ee-ree-mahssh-tah)
I needed (it).

How many do you need? How many do you
want?
Ikutsu irimasu ka?
(ee-koot-sue ee-ree-mahss kah)

Do you need this? Do you want this?
Kore ga irimasu ka?
(koe-ray gah ee-ree-mahss kah)

No, I don't want it.
Irimasen.
(ee-ree-mah-sen)

73. **wakaru**   (wah-kah-rue)
to understand, know

Wakarimasu.   (wah-kah-ree-mahss)
I understand.
Wakarimasen.   (wah-kah-ree-mah-sen)
I do not understand.
Wakarimasu ka?   (wah-kah-ree-mahss kah)
Do you understand?
Wakarimashita.   (wah-kah-ree-mahssh-tah)
I understood. I understand.

Did you understand (me)?

Wakarimashita ka?
(wah-kah-ree-mahssh-tah kah)

I did not understand.
Wakarimasen deshita.
(wah-kah-ree-mah-sen dessh-tah)

Do you know her name?
Ano hito no namae ga wakarimasu ka?
(ah-no-ssh-toe no nah-my gah wah-ka-ree-mahss kah)

No, I don't know (it).
Wakarimasen.
(wah-kah-ree-mah-sen)

74. **ban / bangō**   (bahn) / (bahn-go)
number / numbers

There are two sets of numbers in Japanese. One set (made up of original Japanese terms) goes only from one through ten. The other set, adopted from China, is complete.

JAPANESE

1   hitotsu (he-toe-t'sue)

2 **futatsu** (fuu-tah-t'sue)
3 **mittsu** (meet-sue)
4 **yottsu** (yoat-sue)
5 **itsutsu** (eat-sue-t'sue)
6 **muttsu** (moot-sue)
7 **nanatsu** (nah-nah-t'sue)
8 **yattsu** (yaht-sue)
9 **kokonotsu** (koe-koe-no-t'sue)
10 **tō** (toe)

CHINESE

1 **ichi** (ee-chee)
2 **ni** (nee)
3 **san** (sahn)
4 **shi** (she), **yon** (yoan)
5 **go** (go)
6 **roku** (roe-koo)
7 **shichi** (she-chee), **nana** (nah-nah),
8 **hachi** (hah-chee)
9 **ku** (koo), **kyū** (cue)
10 **jū** (joo)

After ten only the Chinese numbers are used. Eleven is a combination of ten plus one *(jū-ichi)*, twelve is ten plus two *(jū-ni)*, and so on. Twenty is two tens *(ni-jū)*, thirty is three tens *(san-jū)*, and so on.

11	jū-ichi	102	hyaku-ni
12	jū-ni	120	hyaku-ni-jū
13	jū-san	121	hyaku-ni-jū-ichi
14	jū-yon	130	hyaku-san-jū
15	jū-go	200	ni-hyaku
16	jū-roku	300	san-byaku (b'yah-koo)
17	jū-shichi, jū-nana	600	roppyaku (rope-p'yah-koo)
18	jū-hachi	800	happyaku (hop-p'yah-koo)
19	jū-kyū	1,000	sen, issen (ee-ssen)
20	ni-jū	1,100	sen-hyaku
21	ni-jū-ichi	1,200	sen-ni-hyaku
22	ni-jū-ni	2,000	ni-sen
25	ni-jū-go	3,000	san-zen
30	san-jū	5,000	go-sen
31	san-jū-ichi	8,000	hassen (hah-ssen)
32	san-jū-ni	10,000	ichi-man (ee-chee-mahn)
40	yon-jū	11,000	ichi-man-issen
50	go-jū	15,000	ichi-man-go-sen
60	roku-jū	20,000	ni-man
70	shichi-jū, nana-jū	50,000	go-man
80	hachi-jū	100,000	jū-man
90	kyū-jū, ku-jū	200,000	ni-jū-man
100	hyaku (h'yah-koo)	500,000	go-jū-man
101	hyaku-ichi	1,000,000	hyaku-man

75. **hitori** (ssh-toe-ree)
one person

When referring to one or two persons, a form of the Japanese counting system is used.

76. **futari** (fuu-tah-ree)
two persons

(We are) two persons.
Futari desu.
(fuu-tah-ree dess)

From three persons on up, the usual number system is used when counting people. When you enter a restaurant, the host will use *nan mei sama?* (nahn may sah-mah) to ask, "How many persons?" In this instance *nan* means "how many" instead of "what," *mei* is another way of saying "person," and *sama* is an honorific form of *san*. If you are a party of two you can answer *futari desu* or *ni mei desu*.

77. **san nin** (sahn neen)
three persons

(We are) three persons.
San nin desu.
(sahn neen dess)

78. yonin   (yo-neen)
four persons

(We are) four persons.
Yonin desu.
(yo-neen dess)

79. jikan   (jee-kahn)
time, hour

ichi-jikan	one hour
ni-jikan	two hours
san-jikan	three hours
yo-jikan	four hours
go-jikan	five hours, etc.

Time is expressed the following way.

ichi-ji	one o'clock
ni-ji	two o'clock
san-ji	three o'clock
yo-ji	four o'clock
go-ji	five o'clock
roku-ji	six o'clock
shichi-ji	seven o'clock
hachi-ji	eight o'clock

ku-ji	nine o'clock
jū-ji	ten o'clock
jū-ichi-ji	eleven o'clock
jū-ni-ji	twelve o'clock

80. **fun / pun**   (hoon / poon)
minute, minutes

ippun   (eep-poon)
one minute
ni-fun   (nee-hoon)
two minutes
san-pun   (sahn-poon)
three minutes
yon-pun   (yoan-poon)
four minutes
go-fun   (go-hoon)
five minutes
roppun   (rope-poon)
six minutes
shichi-fun   (she-chee-hoon)
seven minutes
hachi-fun   (hah-chee-hoon)
eight minutes
kyū-fun   (cue-hoon)
nine minutes

juppun (joop-poon)
ten minutes
jū-ippun (juu-eep-poon)
eleven minutes
jū-ni-fun (juu-nee-hoon)
twelve minutes
ni-juppun (nee-joop-poon)
twenty minutes
san-juppun (sahn-joop-poon)
thirty minutes
yon-jū-go-fun (yoan-joo-go-hoon)
forty-five minutes, etc.

• • • • • • • • **JAPANESE DIALECTS** • • • • • • • •

Students of the Japanese language and especially short-term visitors who attempt to learn just enough to get by, generally do not have to worry about Japanese dialects because virtually all Japanese understand *hyōjungo* (h'yoe-june-go) which is the standard language spoken in Tōkyō.

However, even beginning students of the language will immediately pick up on differences in the accents and vocabulary of residents of Tōkyō, Kyōto, Ōsaka, Kōbe, and other cities. Dialects that are basically unintelligible to students of standard Japanese include those spoken in

84

Kagoshima on the southern end of Kyūshū island and Aomori in northeastern Honshū (the main island).

There are dozens of other regional dialects different enough that the speakers are instantly recognizable as natives of certain areas. Some of these dialects are so different from standard Japanese that even Japanese people who are not from those areas have difficulty understanding what is being said.

• •

PART 9

Words 81–90

81. **gozen**   (go-zen)
    morning (AM)

82. **gogo**   (go-go)
    afternoon (PM)

It is ten-thirty in the morning.
Gozen no jū-ji san-juppun desu.
(go-zen no juu-jee sahn-joop-poon dess)

I will meet you this afternoon at two o'clock.
Kyō no gogo ni-ji ni aimasu.
(k'yoe no go-go nee-jee nee aye-mahss)

Let's go this afternoon.
Kyō no gogo ni ikimashō.
(k'yoe no go-go nee ee-kee-mah-show)

Let's go tomorrow afternoon.

Ashita no gogo ni ikimashō.
(ahssh-tah no go-go nee ee-kee-mah-show)

83. **takushii** (tahk-she)
   taxi

   I want to go by taxi.
   Takushii de ikitai desu.
   (tahk-she day ee-kee-tie dess)

   Please call a taxi.
   Takushii wo yonde kudasai.
   (tahk-she oh yoan-day koo-dah-sie)

   Let's go by taxi.
   Takushii de ikimashō.
   (tahk-she day ee-kee-mah-show)

84. **chikatetsu** (chee-kah-tet-sue)
   subway

   Where is the subway?
   Chikatetsu wa doko desu ka?
   (chee-kah-tet-sue wah doe-koe dess kah)

   I want to go by subway.

Chikatetsu de ikitai desu.
(chee-kah-tet-sue day ee-kee-tie dess)

Shall we go by subway?
Chikatetsu de ikimashō ka?
(chee-kah-tet-sue day ee-kee-mah-show kah)

Let's go by subway.
Chikatetsu de ikimashō.
(chee-kah-tet-sue day ee-kee-mah-show)

85. **densha** (den-shah)
train

Shall we go by train?
Densha de ikimashō ka?
(den-shah day ee-kee-mah-show kah)

Let's go by train.
Densha de ikimashō.
(den-shah day ee-kee-mah-show)

Is it better to go by train?
Densha de iku hō ga ii desu ka?
(den-shah day ee-koo hoh gah ee dess kah)

86. eki   (eh-kee)
station

Where is the station?
Eki wa doko desu ka?
(eh-kee wah doe-koe dess kah)

87. chikai   (chee-kie)
near

Where is the nearest subway station?
Ichiban chikai chikatetsu wa doko desu ka?
(ee-chee-bahn chee-kie chee-kah-tet-sue wah
doe-koe dess kah)

How much is the subway from here to the Ginza?
**Koko kara* Ginza made no chikatesu wa ikura
desu ka?**
(koe-koe kah-rah geen-zah mah-day no chee-
kah-tet-sue wah ee-koo-rah dess kah)
*kara (kah-rah) means "from."

88. shinkansen   (sheen-kahn-sen)
bullet train
Bullet trains run at speeds of 200 kph (120 mph).

I want to go by bullet train.
Shinkansen de ikitai desu.
(sheen-kahn-sen day ee-kee-tie dess)

Does the bullet train stop in Yokohama?
Shinkansen wa Yokohama ni tomarimasu ka?
(sheen-kahn-sen wah Yokohama nee toe-mah-ree-mahss kah)

Yes, it does stop (there).
Tomarimasu.
(toe-mah-ree-mahss)

89. **atsui**   (aht-sue-ee)
hot (weather and to the touch)

It is really hot today.
Kyo wa hontō* ni atsui desu.
(k'yoe wah hone-toe nee aht-sue-ee dess)
*Hontō means "real" and hontō ni means "really."

It's hot today, isn't it!
Kyō wa atsui desu ne!
(k'yoe wah aht-sue-ee dess nay)

Is the water hot?

Mizu ga atsui desu ka?
(me-zoo gah aht-sue-ee dess kah)

90. **samui**   (sah-moo-ee)
cold (weather)

It's cold, isn't it!
Samui desu ne!
(sah-moo-ee dess nay)

Are you cold?
Samui desu ka?
(sah-moo-ee dess kah)

No, I'm not cold.
Iie, samuku nai desu.
(eee-eh, sah-moo-koo nie dess)

● ● ● ● ● ● ● **GIVING UP ON JAPANESE** ● ● ● ● ● ● ●

Prior to the dissolution of the Tokugawa shogunate in
1868, Japan was divided into more than 200 fiefs
presided over by hereditary lords called *daimyō* (dime-
yoe), literally "great names." Many of these fiefs func-
tioned more or less as independent kingdoms, with their

91

own unique dialects. Travel was tightly controlled and there was no national mass media to bind the people or languages together.

The diversity of dialects and the difficulty encountered in learning how to write the complicated Chinese characters (adopted between the 4th and 6th centuries A.D.) was such an enormous problem that some of the leaders of the early Meiji period suggested that the nation give up Japanese and adopt English as the official language of the country. Needless to say, this was not a very popular suggestion.

● ●

PART 10

Words 91–100

91. tsumetai (t'sue-may-tie)
cold (to the touch)

This water is cold!
Kono mizu wa tsumetai desu!
(koe-no mee-zoo wah t'sue-may-tie dess)

92. kōhii (koe-hee)
coffee

Hot coffee, please.
Atsui kōhii wo kudasai.
(aht-sue-ee koe-hee oh koo-dah-sie)

Iced coffee, please.
Aisu kōhii wo kudasai.
(eye-sue koe-hee oh koo-dah-sie)

93. **miruku**   (me-rue-koo)
    milk

    Cold milk, please.
    Tsumetai miruku wo kudasai.
    (t'sue-may-tie mee-rue-koo oh koo-dah-sie)

94. **ame**   (ah-may)
    rain

95. **yuki**   (yoo-kee)
    snow

96. **furimasu**   (fuu-ree-mahss)
    to fall, come down, drop

    It is raining.
    Ame ga futte imasu.
    (ah-may gah fuut-tay ee-mahss)

    It is snowing.
    Yuki ga futte imasu.
    (yoo-kee gah fuut-tay ee-mahss)

    Will it rain tomorrow?

Ashita ame ga furimasu ka?
(ahssh-tah ah-may gah fuu-ree-mahss kah)

No, it will not rain.
Iie, furimasen.
(ee-eh, fuu-ree-mah-sen)

97. **byōki** (b'yoe-kee)
sick

98. **o-isha** (oh-ee-shah)
doctor

I'm sick, please call a doctor.
Byōki desu, o-isha wo yonde kudasai.
(b'yoe-kee dess, oh-ee-shah oh yoan-day koo-dah-sie)

99. **aruku** (ah-rue-koo)
to walk

Arukimasu. (ah-rue-kee-mahss)
I will walk.
Arukimasen. (ah-rue-kee-mah-sen)
I will not walk.

Arukimasu ka?   (ah-rue-kee-mahssh kah)
I walked.
Arukitai.   (ah-rue-kee-tie)
I want to walk.
Arukimashō ka?   (ah-rue-kee-mah-show kah)
Shall we walk?
Arukimashō.   (ah-rue-kee-mah-show)
Let's walk.
Arukimashita.   (ah-rue-kee-mahssh-tah)
I walked.

100. tōi   (toy)
far, distant

Is it (very) far?
Tōi desu ka?
(toy dess kah)

Is it all right to walk from here?
Koko kara aruite mo ii desu ka?
(koe-koe kah-rah ah-rue-ee-tay moh ee dess kah)

No, it is (too) far.
Iie, tōi desu.
(eee-eh, toy dess)

No, it is not far.
Iie, tōku nai desu.
(eee-eh, toe-koo nie dess)

• • • • • •   **THOSE *KANJI* CHARACTERS**   • • • • • •

Altogether there are well over 30,000 Chinese characters, but only a small percentage of this number are
commonly used today. Successive language reforms that
began in Japan shortly after the fall of the Tokugawa
shogunate in 1868 have greatly reduced the number of
kanji (kahn-jee) taught in schools and used for official
purposes.

The last reform occurred in 1981, when the number of
characters was officially set at 1,945. This list is referred
to as the *jōyō kanji* (joe-yoe kahn-jee) or "Chinese
Characters for Daily Use." Children are required to learn
a total of 1,006 characters during their first six years of
school.

Special Set Phrases

There are a number of set expressions in Japanese that are an important part of the country's formal etiquette system. These terms are used daily and contribute significantly to the flavor of the culture. Using them adds a very polite and natural nuance to your speech.

Irasshaimase! (ee-rah-shy-mah-say)
Welcome!

Tadaima! (tah-die-mah)
I'm home! (I've returned!)

O-kaeri nasai! (oh-kie-eh-ree nah-sie)
Welcome back (home)!

O-jama shimasu. (oh-jah-mah she-mahss)
I am intruding. Excuse me.
This is a polite term used when you enter someone's home, office, or private room.

O-jama shimashita.   (oh-jah-mah she-mahssh-tah)

I have intruded. I have bothered you. Goodbye.

This is said when you leave a home or office you have been visiting.

Shitsurei shimasu.   (sheet-sue-ray she-mahss)

Excuse me. I'm sorry.

This term is used when you pass in front of someone (as in a theater or while walking through a crowd). It is also used when entering someone's office, as an apology for disturbing him or her.

Shitsurei shimashita.   (sheet-sue-ray she-mahssh-tah)

Sorry for disturbing (bothering) you.

This is said when you interfere with some person or situation (as when you bump into someone, mistakenly walk into an office or meeting room that is being used, or cause any kind of minor disturbance).

Itadakimasu.   (ee-tah-dah-kee-mahss)

Bon appetite. (receive, accept)

Mentioned earlier in the **100 Key Word section** as "I will receive (something)," this term is regularly used just before beginning to eat or drink, especially when someone else is the host, but also by family members in their own home. It is a courteous expression of thanks and appreciation and, although it is not religious in nature, it has the same ritualistic feel as the saying of grace before a meal.

O-somatsu sama. (oh-so-maht-sue sah-mah)
It was nothing.

When you have a meal at a private home and thank the cook, this is the term he or she is most likely to use in response. Its figurative meaning is "It was nothing, but thank you for mentioning it."

O-kage sama de. (oh-kah-gay sah-mah day)
Thanks to you. Thank you for asking.

This is often said as a response when someone asks you how you are, or how a friend or family member is doing, or how things are going. In essence it means "Thank you for asking . . ." and is followed by "I'm doing fine," "He or she is fine," etc.

Gokurō sama. (goe-koo-roe sah-mah)
Thanks for all your hard work. Well done.

This ceremonial expression literally means something like "honorable one who went to a great deal of trouble, who went above and beyond the call of duty to accomplish some task." It is commonly used as a way of expressing thanks to someone who worked hard and is finished for the day.

O-negai shimasu.   (oh-nay-guy she-mahss)
O-negai itashimasu.   (oh-nay-guy ee-tah-she-mahss)
Please (do something for the speaker).

These polite terms are used, virtually interchangeably, when asking a favor from someone or some kind of special consideration or help. The "please" connotation is very strong, as in "I beg of you." They are complete sentences within themselves and are generally used after the speaker has asked the other party to do something or accept some obligation.

Yoroshiku o-negai shimasu.   (yoe-roe-she-koo oh-nay-guy she-mahss)
Yoroshiku o-negai itashimasu.   (yoe-roe-she-koo oh-nay-guy ee-tah-shee-mahss)
Please (do something for the speaker).
(very polite)

Both *o-negai shimasu* and *o-negai itashimasu* are commonly preceeded by *yoroshiku* (yoe-roe-she-koo) and a bow, which significantly increases the power of the request and turns it into a serious appeal.

Common Everyday Expressions

O-genki desu ka?   (oh-gen-kee dess kah)
How are you? Are you well?

Genki desu. Anata wa?   (gen-kee dess ah-nah-tah wah)
I'm fine. And you?

O-tenki wa ii desu ne!   (oh-ten-kee wah eee dess nay)
The weather is fine, isn't it!

Chotto o-machi kudasai.   (choat-toe oh-mah-chee koo-dah-sie)
Just a moment, please.

Chotto matte!   (choat-toe maht-tay)
Just a second! Hang on! (informal)

Dōitashimashite.   (doe-ee-tah-she-mahssh-tay)
Don't mention it. You're welcome.

Hajimemashite.   (hah-jee-may-mahssh-tay)
Pleased to meet you.

Additional Vocabulary

(A)
address jūsho (juu-show)
age toshi (toe-she)
air-conditioning eā kon (ay-ah kone)
airmail kōkūbin (koe-koo-bean)
airplane hikōki (he-koe-kee)
airport kūkō (koo-koe)
April shigatsu (she-got-sue)
arrive tsukimasu (t'sue-kee-mahss)
August hachigatsu (hah-chee-got-sue)
automobile jidōsha (jee-doe-shah)

(B)
bank ginkō (geen-koe)
bar bā (bah)
bath o-furo (oh-fuu-roe)
beautiful utsukushii (oo-t'sue-koo-shee)
beef biifu (bee-fuu)

birthday tanjōbi (tahn-joe-bee)
book hon (hone)
bookstore hon'ya (hone-yah)
box lunch (Japanese-style) o-bentō (oh-ben-toe)
bread pan (pahn)
breakfast asagohan (ah-sah-go-hahn)
bridge hashi (hah-she)
building biru (be-rue)
bus basu (bah-sue)

(C)
cabaret kyabare (k'yah-bah-ray)
camera kamera (kah-may-rah)
car kuruma (koo-rue-mah)
chair isu (ee-sue)
change (money returned) o-tsuri (oh-t'sue-ree)
change (small coins) komakai-no (koe-mah-kie-no)
children kodomo (koe-doe-moe)
chopsticks o-hashi (oh-hah-she)
cold (illnes) kaze (kah-zay)
   catch a cold kaze wo hikimasu (kah-zay oh he-kee-mahss)
congratulations omedetō gozaimasu (oh-may-day-toe go-zie-mahss)
corner kado (kah-doe)
cover charge kabā chāji (kah-bah chah-jee)

(D)

date (time of the month) hizuke (he-zoo-kay)
daughter musume (moo-sue-may)
daytime hiruma (he-rue-mah)
day after tomorrow asatte (ah-saht-tay)
December jūnigatsu (juu-nee-got-sue)
deliver todokemasu (toe-doe-kay-mahss)
dentist haisha (hie-shah)
departure shuppatsu (shupe-pot-sue)
deposit (for room) tekin (tay-keen)
dessert dezāto (day-zah-toe)
dining car shokudō sha (show-koo-doe shah)
dining room shokudō (show-koo-doe)
dinner (evening meal) yūshoku (yuu-show-koo)
drink nomimono (no-me-moe-no)
discount waribiki (wah-ree-bee-kee)
dollar doru (doe-rue)
double room daburu (dah-boo-rue)
driver untenshu (oon-ten-shoo)
drugstrore yakkyoku (yahk-k'yoe-koo)
dry cleaning dorai kuriiningu (doe-rye koo-ree-neen-goo)

(E)

east higashi (he-gah-she)
eel unagi (oo-nah-ghee)

embassy taishikan (tie-she-kahn)

egg tamago (tah-mah-go)

England Eikoku (a-e-koe-koo)

entrance iriguchi (ee-ree-goo-chee)

evening yūgata (yuu-gah-tah)
   this evening komban (kome-bahn)

exit deguchi (day-goo-chee)

express train kyūkō (cue-koe)

expressway (highway) kōsokudōro (koe-soe-koo-doe-roe)

eye me (may)

eyeglasses megane (may-gah-nay)

(F)

fall (season) aki (ah-kee)

February nigatsu (nee-got-sue)

fee tesūryō (tay-sue-r'yoe)

festival o-matsuri (oh-maht-sue-ree)

fever netsu (neh-t'sue)

first-class (tickets) ittō (eet-toe)

fish sakana (sah-kah-nah)

foreign gaikoku (guy-koe-koo)

foreigner gaikokujin (guy-koe-koo-jeen)

France Furansu (fuu-rahn-sue)

front desk furonto (fuu-roan-toe)

fruit kudamono (koo-dah-moe-no)

107

(G)

gallery gyararii (g'yah-rah-ree)
garden niwa (nee-wah)
garlic ninniku (neen-nee-koo)
genuine honmono no (home-moe-no no)
Germany Doitsu (doe-ee-t'sue)
get off (disembark) orimasu (oh-ree-mahss)
get on (board) norimasu (no-ree-mahss)
gram guramu (goo-rah-moo)
guest o-kyaku (oh-k'yah-koo)

(H)

hand te (tay)
hanger (for clothing) hangā (hahn-gah)
heart attack shinzō mahi (sheen-zoe mah-hee)
heavy omoi (owe-moy)
holiday yasumi no hi (yah-sue-me no hee)
home uchi (oo-chee)
horseradish wasabi (wah-sah-bee)
hospital byōin (b'yoe-een)
hostess hosutesu (hoe-sue-tay-sue)
hot (spicy) karai (kah-rye)
hotspring onsen (own-sen)
house (structure) ie (ee-eh)
hungry onaka ga sukimasu (oh-nah-kah gah ski-mahss)

hurry   isogimasu   (ee-so-ghee-mahss)
hurt (pain)   itai   (ee-tie)

(I)
inn (Japanese style)   ryokan   (r'yoe-kahn)
international   kokusai   (coke-sie)
international telephone (call)   kokusai denwa   (koke-sie den-wah)
intersection   kōsaten   (koe-sah-ten)
introduce   shōkai shimasu   (show-kie she-mahss)
introduction   shōkaijo   (show-kie-joe)

(J)
January   ichigatsu   (ee-chee-got-sue)
Japan   Nihon   (nee-hone)
Japanese-style bed   futon   (fuu-tone)
Japanese-style room   nihon-ma   (nee-hone-mah)
job   shigoto   (she-go-toe)
July   shichigatsu   (she-chee-got-sue)
June   rokugatsu   (roe-koo-got-sue)

(K)
key   kagi   (kah-ghee)
kilogram   kiro   (kee-roe)
kilometer   kiro   (kee-roe)
kind (nice)   shinsetsu   (shin-set-sue)

Korea Kankoku (kahn-koe-koo)
Korean (language) Kankokugo (kahn-koe-koo-go)
Korean (person) Kankoku-jin (kahn-koe-koo-jeen)

(L)
last (final) saigo (sie-go)
last day saigo no hi (sie-go no hee)
last month sengetsu (sen-get-sue)
last week senshū (sen-shoo)
last year kyonen (k'yoe-nen)
laundry sentakumono (sen-tah-koo-moe-no)
left (direction/side) hidari (he-dah-ree)
letter tegami (teh-gah-me)
luggage nimotsu (nee-moat-sue)
lunch hirugohan (he-rue-go-hahn)

(M)
maid meido (may-e-doe)
man (male) otoko (oh-toe-koe)
manager manējā (mah-nay-jah)
map chizu (chee-zoo)
March sangatsu (sahn-got-sue)
May gogatsu (go-got-sue)
meal ticket shokken (shoke-ken)
meat niku (nee-koo)
medicine kusuri (koo-sue-ree)

menu menyū (men-yuu)
morning asa (ah-sah)
movie eiga (a-e-gah)

(N)
name card meishi (may-she)
napkin napukin (nahp-keen)
New Year's o-shogatsu (oh-show-got-sue)
next tsugi (t'sue-ghee)
next month raigetsu (rye-get-sue)
next week raishū (rye-shoo)
next year rainen (rye-nen)
night yoru (yoe-rue)
nightclub naito kurabu (nie-toe koo-rah-boo)
north kita (kee-tah)
November jūichigatsu (juu-ee-chee-got-sue)

(O)
October jūgatsu (juu-got-sue)
once ichido (ee-chee-doe)
one-way (street) ippō tsūkō (eep-poe t'sue-koe)
one-way (ticket) kata-michi (kah-tah-mee-chee)
onions tamanegi (tah-mah-nay-ghee)

(P)
package (parcel) kozutsumi (koe-zoot-sue-me)

111

paper kami (kah-me)
park (recreational area) kōen (koe-en)
parking lot chūshajō (choo-shah-joe)
passport pasupōto (pah-sue-poe-toe)
pearls shinju (sheen-juu)
pepper koshō (koe-show)
platform (train) hōmu (hoe-moo)
police box (small sub-station on street) kōban (koe-bahn)
policeman o-mawari-san (oh-mah-wah-ree-sahn)
porter pōtā (poe-tah)
post office yūbin kyoku (yuu-bean k'yoe-koo)
potatoes jagaimo (jah-guy-ee-moe)
pottery tōki (toe-kee)
public telephone kōshū denwa (koe-shoo den-wah)

(R)
refrigerator reizōko (ray-e-zoe-koe)
refund harai-modoshi (hah-rye-moe-doe-she)
rent yachin (yah-cheen)
repair naoshimasu (nah-oh-she-mahss)
reservation yoyaku (yoe-yah-koo)
reserved seat shiteiseki (ssh-tay-seh-kee)
restaurant (Japanese) ryōriya (rio-ree-yah)
restaurant (Western) resutoran (res-toe-ran)
rice (cooked white rice) gohan (go-hahn)

right (direction/side) migi (mee-ghee)
road michi (mee-chee)
room heya (hay-yah)
room (Japanese-style) nihon-ma (nee-hone-mah)
room (Western-style) yōma (yoe-mah)
room number rūmu nambā (rue-moo nahm-bah)
room service rūmu sābisu (rue-moo sah-bee-sue)

(S)
salt shio (she-oh)
schedule (plan) yotei (yoe-tay)
school gakkō (gahk-koe)
sea (ocean) umi (oo-me)
seamail funabin (fuu-nah-bean)
seasick funayoi (fuu-nah-yoe-e)
seaside kaigan (kie-gahn)
season kisetsu (kee-set-sue)
seat seki (seh-kee)
seat number seki no nambā (seh-kee no nahm-bah)
September kugatsu (koo-got-sue)
service center sābisu sentā (sah-bee-sue sen-tah)
ship fune (fuu-nay)
shirt shātsu (shah-t'sue)
shrine jinja (jeen-jah)
single room shinguru (sheen-goo-rue)
slow yukkuri (yuke-koo-ree)

soap sekken (sek-ken)
son musuko (moose-koe)
south minami (me-nah-me)
souvenir (gift) omiyage (oh-me-yah-gay)
soy sauce shōyu (show-yoo)
spicy karai (kah-rye)
spoon supūn (su-poon)
spring haru (hah-rue)
stamp (for mail) kitte (keet-tay)
stop (bus/train) teiryūjo (tay-e-r'yoo-joe)
straight (direction) massugu (mahss-sue-goo)
sugar satō (sah-toe)
summer natsu (not-sue)
supermarket sūpā (sue-pah)

(T)
table tēburu (tay-boo-rue)
tag (label) harigami (hah-ree-gah-me)
taxi stand takushii noriba (tah-koo-she no-ree-bah)
tea (black/brown) kōcha (koe-chah)
tea (Japanese green tea) nihon-cha (nee-hone-chah)
television terebi (tay-ray-bee)
temperature (body) taion (tie-own)
temperature (weather) ondo (own-doe)
temple o-tera (oh-tay-rah)
theater (movies) eigakan (a-e-gah-kahn)

ticket kippu (keep-poo)
ticket window (vending machines) kippu uriba (keep-poo oo-ree-bah)
toilet o-tearai (oh-tay-ah-rye)
tonight komban (kome-bahn)
traffic kōtsū (kote-sue)
traffic light shingō (sheen-go)
traveler's checks toraberāzu chekku (toe-rah-bay-rah-zoo check-ku)
twin room (two persons, two beds) tsuin (t'sue-ween)

(V)
vegetables yasai (yah-sie)
visa biza (bee-zah)

(W)
waiter ūetā (way-tah)
washroom o-tearai (oh-tay-ah-rye)
way (direction) iku michi (ee-koo me-chee)
weather tenki (ten-kee)
weather forecast tenki yohō (ten-kee yoe-hoe)
west nishi (nee-she)
window mado (mah-doe)
winter fuyu (fuu-yoo)
women onna no hito (own-nah no ssh-toe)
wonderful subarashii (sue-bah-rah-she)

(Y)

yesterday kinō (kee-no)
young wakai (wah-kie)
youth hostel yūsu hosuteru (yoo-sue hos-tay-rue)

Z)

zoo dōbutsuen (doe-boot-sue-en)

NOTES